WHAT TO SERVE
YOUR SHADOW KING

A TOAST TO BITTER
RIVALS

FRUITS OF THE FAE

SCRUMPTIOUS
SPRITZES

TOE-CURLING TIPPLES

SERIOUS SPICE & SLOW
BURNERS

GW00569390

A COUPE
OF THORNS
AND ROSÉ

A COUPE OF THORNS AND ROSÉ

Romantasy Cocktails to Quench Your Thirst

POP PRESS

WHAT TO SERVE
YOUR SHADOW KING

A TOAST TO BITTER
RIVALS

FRUITS OF THE FAE

SCRUMPTIOUS
SPRITZES

TOE-CURLING TIPPLES

SERIOUS SPICE & SLOW
BURNERS

Contents

WHAT TO SERVE YOUR SHADOW KING

Old-Fashioned Alpha Male 9

Morally Greyhound 11

The Cruel Quince Daiquiri 13

The Wicked Sling 15

Vampiro 17

Beast Between The Sheets 19

Mai Tai-rant 21

Fine, Make Me Your Vesper 23

Green-eyed Fairy 25

The Devil Within Me 27

A TOAST TO BITTER RIVALS

She's Got A Concealed Weapon 31

Viscous Little Thing 33

Once Upon a Bramble Heart 35

The Ballad of Negroni After 37

Girl, Goddess, Gibson 39

Grumpy Wants Tequila Sunshine 41

Brandy Banter 42

The Gauntlet Gimlet 45

The Aperol Six 47

Magical Manhattan.................. 49

FRUITS OF THE FAE

Bloody Fairy 53

Smash Me 55

The Priory of the Orange-tini 59

High Lady 61

Crescent City Cosmopolitan 63

Flame House Punch 65

You Hit Me Like a Hurricane 67

Pine After Colada 69

Ninth Cocktail...................... 71

Cursed Forest Mojito 73

SCRUMPTIOUS SPRITZES

A Coupe of Thorns and Rosé........... 77

Mortal Mule 79

Mourning Glory Fizz 80

Shape-shifter Spritz.................. 81

The Kir of Nothing.................. 83

Ambrosia........................ 85

Scarlet Collins 87

Hunt Me on Dark and Stormy Waters.... 89

A Marvellous, Light Lemonade. 93
A Twinkle of Frost and Starlight 95

TOE-CURLING TIPPLES

Hair of the Wolf. 101
Little Scorpion. 103
'Nogkiller. 105
Empyrean Espresso Martini. 107
Ale of Twin Cities 108
Randy Alexandrian 111
One Hell of a Sour. 113
Saints Au Champagne. 115
A Violent End in the Afternoon 117
White Lies. 118

SERIOUS SPICE AND SLOW BURNERS

Black Velvet Wing 123
Love or Burnt Martini 125
Juleps on Mine. 127
Greedy G&T 131
Dragon's Scale Ale 133
Spice and Sloe 135
Sloe Burn 137
Blood and Smut 139
House of Hanky Panky 143
Dragon Margarider 144

Introduction

IT'S ALL ABOUT THE CHEMISTRY

What is it that makes the perfect romantasy? And, while we are here, what about the perfect cocktail? Perhaps there's a crossover between the two. Neither should be too sweet or cloying. But neither do we want elements that are eternally at odds – there is such a thing as too much tension! Perhaps it's about balance then, about all the ingredients – cough – coming together to create something that's truly magical.

From martinis to highballs and sours to snappers, it's hard to explain why some cocktails have swept the globe. Maybe we shouldn't try – just like we don't need to understand exactly what it is that makes our toes curl about stories filled with morally grey characters, mythical creatures and more than a little death. Perhaps the allure is just as instinctual as falling for your mate. And happily, that is what this book is here to do! In these pages you will find 60 cocktails inspired by our favourite romantasy stories. Some may be familiar, some may seem worlds apart from our own, but this is a genre all about discovery. So whether you're into fairies, vampires, demons or dragons, just like cocktails, there is one out there for everyone.

The greatest romantasy reads take well-loved tropes – enemies to lovers, grumpy vs. sunshine, reverse harems – and make them their own. Sure, the fated couple have to navigate a few obstacles and warring kingdoms first, but with a generous dose of smut these books create a love so powerful it transcends the page and connects readers everywhere. Is there anything more pleasurable than lighting some candles, curling up in your book nook and escaping to your favourite realm? Maybe it's adding some extra spice to your bookclub and sitting down to scream, laugh (or maybe cry!) together about *those* chapters? It could be a date, a group of friends, your BFF (but absolutely not your parents) – introducing them to your favourite series or standalone only enhances the connection. And what better way to set the scene than by making a cocktail to settle down with first?

Whatever you like in a main character – whether you prefer a stabby heroine, a golden retriever pirate captain or a dark fairy with an *enormous* wing span – you will find it all on the page. No date can be so awkward, no working day so dull, no night so dark and lonely that a romantasy novel can't make your stomach do somersaults. So let's raise a glass to whatever cocktail piques your interest and make a toast: here's to finding your book boyfriend (or if we're being honest, *boyfriends*). All the cocktails in this recipe book are made for a single serving unless stated otherwise but you can of course multiply up depending on how many you're serving. Glassware is also a suggestion so don't let a lack of specific glassware stop you from having fun! And as sugar syrup is a common ingredient, below is an easy guide to make your own.

HOW TO MAKE YOUR OWN SUGAR SYRUP

Essentially this is just sugar and water and all the recipes in this book require a mix in the ratio of 1:1 by volume. However, if you do see the use of 2:1 for other recipes, that simply means using double the sugar to the water. You can make these easily at home and create a batch so you have it to hand when you fancy a drink.

A 1:1 mix can be made using a blender; just add equal volumes of water and sugar to a blender and blend until well mixed.

To make a 2:1 syrup you will generally need heat to ensure the sugar dissolves in the water. Heat the water gently in a pan, then add half of the sugar. Stir briefly and leave until the mixture becomes clear. Add the remaining sugar and repeat. Be careful not to over-stir; the mixture will clarify on its own if left, without agitation.

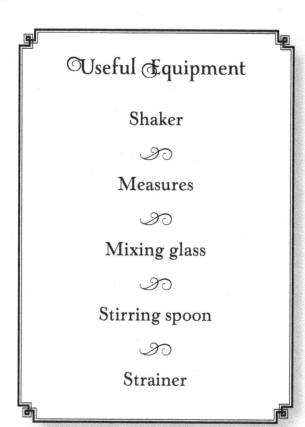

Useful Equipment

Shaker

Measures

Mixing glass

Stirring spoon

Strainer

WHAT TO SERVE YOUR SHADOW KING

Old-Fashioned Alpha Male

Bride by Ali Hazelwood

Have you found yourself alone with the big, bad wolf? There are only two ways this can go, much the same as this strong yet complex cocktail. So take a sip, settle down with *Bride* and get ready to go feral.

Ingredients

10ml sugar syrup or a bar spoon
(long-handled mixing spoon) of sugar
2–3 dashes Angostura bitters
50ml golden or dark rum

Glassware: Rocks glass

Add a large disc of orange zest to the bottom of a rocks glass along with the sugar syrup, bitters and 25ml of the rum. Add two cubes of ice and stir 20–30 times to mix. Add the remaining rum and two more ice cubes and stir again.

Put the sugar and the bitters into a rocks glass. Add a few drops of rum and stir with a spoon to dissolve the sugar. Add 25ml of the rum to the glass along with two cubes of ice and stir 20–30 times to mix. Add a large disc of orange zest, the remaining rum and two more ice cubes before stirring again.

MORALLY GREYHOUND

A COURT THIS CRUEL AND LOVELY
BY STACIA STARK

Completely indifferent to the sweet or sour flavour dichotomy, the Morally Greyhound is the tart cocktail of your dreams. The ambiguity lies in the pink grapefruit juice, which, like everyone's favourite book boyfriend Lorian, has the ability to make you scream for completely opposing reasons. Feel free to use either vodka or gin in this recipe, we really couldn't care less.

INGREDIENTS

50ml vodka or gin
200ml pink grapefruit juice

Glassware: Collins glass

Fill the glass with ice then add the gin or vodka. Pour over the grapefruit juice then stir using a bar spoon. Garnish with a slice of pink grapefruit on the side.

THE CRUEL
QUINCE DAIQUIRI

THE CRUEL PRINCE BY HOLLY BLACK

In a concoction befitting Holly Black's high cheek-
boned antagonist, razor-sharp quince and lime give
way to the irresistible charm of sugar and rum. Take
this as fair warning; no good comes to the girl who
tastes this deceptively delicate cocktail.

INGREDIENTS

50ml white rum
25g quince conserve
20ml lime juice
15ml sugar syrup

Glassware: Martini glass or Champagne coupe

Add all the ingredients to a cocktail shaker. Shake hard
over ice until well mixed (you may need to stir afterwards to ensure the conserve is fully dissolved into the other
ingredients). Double-strain into a chilled Martini glass or
Champagne coupe. Classically the Daiquiri is garnished
with a lime wedge on the rim of the glass, but perhaps faerie
fruit might better suit your purposes . . .

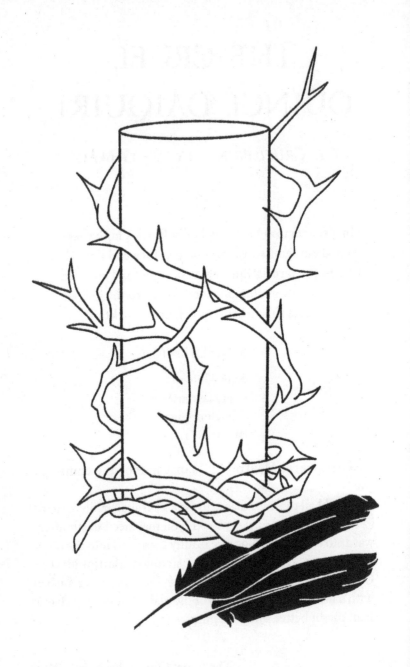

THE WICKED SLING

THE WICKED KING BY HOLLY BLACK

Back for more, are we? Unsurprising really. Despite your complicated feelings, you're as bound to this boozy cocktail as you are to the new – and equally boozy – High King. So better drink this series in, you'll never get sick of it.

INGREDIENTS

30ml gin
7.5ml Cointreau
7.5ml Benedictine
15ml Heering cherry liqueur
15ml lime juice
10ml grenadine
1 dash Angostura bitters
120ml pineapple juice

Glassware: Highball or sling glass

Add all the ingredients to a cocktail shaker. Add ice, shake and strain into a highball or sling glass over ice. Serve with a fruit slice (orange or lemon) and a maraschino cherry.

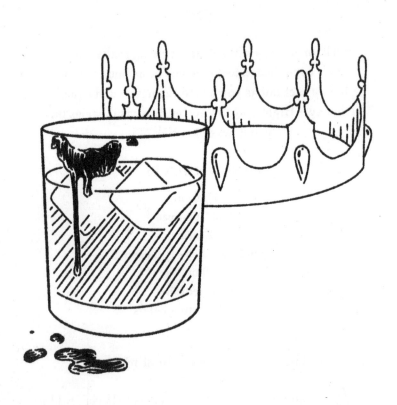

Vampiro

THE SERPENT AND THE WINGS OF NIGHT
BY CARISSA BROADBENT

Heroine Oraya knows all too well the dangers – and
delights – of a bloodthirsty lover. With sweet,
savoury and spice forming an unholy alliance in this
succulent tipple, you just might find out too.

INGREDIENTS

60ml tequila reposado
30ml tomato juice
30ml orange juice
15ml lime juice
15ml grenadine syrup
7 drops of hot pepper sauce
Pinch of salt
Grind of black pepper

Glassware: Old-Fashioned glass

Fill a cocktail shaker with ice. Add all the ingredients and
shake until cold. Strain into an Old-Fashioned glass
filled with ice and add a lime wedge as garnish.

BEAST BETWEEN THE SHEETS

LEDGE BY STACEY MCEWAN

This cocktail is a little unusual in that it mixes two different species – sorry – spirits! It therefore has some serious teeth to it (or should we say talons), yet when made properly, it is a well-balanced and smooth libation. And if Ryon is anything to go by, being unusual only makes you more swoon-worthy.

INGREDIENTS

20ml white rum
20ml Cognac
20ml Cointreau
10ml lemon juice

Glassware: Martini glass or Champagne coupe

Add all the ingredients to a cocktail shaker. Add ice and shake well. Double-strain into your glass, which must be chilled to a glacial temperature. Garnish with a strip of twisted lemon zest.

MAI TAI-RANT

GILD BY RAVEN KENNEDY

Like King Midas himself, it'd be easy to mistake the
Mai Tai for an easy-going, light and fruity cocktail,
a fitting beverage for a guest of his majesty. But in
reality, it's a strong, rum-based tiki-style drink most
suited to dark or golden rum, with bold-as-brass
flavour. The garnish of the half lime carcass serves as
fair warning: its superficial sweetness will be used
against you.

INGREDIENTS

30ml Jamaican gold rum
30ml agricole rum
30ml lime juice
15ml curaçao
10ml orgeat syrup
10ml sugar syrup

Glassware: Rocks glass

Add all the ingredients to a cocktail shaker. Add
crushed or cracked ice and shake well. Strain into a
rocks glass filled with ice and garnish with half of the 'spent'
lime and a mint sprig.

FINE, MAKE ME YOUR VESPER

SHADOW AND BONE BY LEIGH BARDUGO

Best served as cold as you can possibly get it, this is a classic cocktail just as powerful as *Shadow and Bone*'s insatiable villain, the Darkling. Don't forget the lemon twist over the top to add some much-needed citrus sunshine.

INGREDIENTS

60ml gin
20ml vodka
10ml Lillet Blanc

Glassware: Martini glass, goblet or wine glass

Shake all the ingredients with ice in a shaker, and double-strain into a chilled Martini glass, goblet or wine glass. Add a lemon twist over the top to provide the drink with lift from the citrus oils.

GREEN-EYED FAIRY

A COURT OF THORNS AND ROSES
BY SARAH J. MAAS

Oh Tamlin. What lies behind that glittering mask of gold and emerald, behind those piercing green eyes? Impossible beast or handsome young warrior, serve this iconic tipple and you might just find out.

INGREDIENTS

25ml absinthe
25ml chilled water
25ml lemon juice
20ml sugar syrup
1 dash Angostura bitters
½ egg white

Glassware: Martini glass or Champagne coupe

Add all the ingredients to a cocktail shaker. Shake without ice (dry shake), then add ice and shake again (wet shake). Strain into a chilled Martini glass or Champagne coupe. Garnish with a twist of lemon zest or, if you like, a sprinkling of gold edible glitter as a delicious homage to the High Lord who started it all.

THE DEVIL WITHIN ME

ONE DARK WINDOW BY RACHEL GILLIG

Diligent readers will now be well versed in what to serve any seductive villain who darkens your door. But what tipple do you turn to when the monster might actually be you? Known in Mexico as 'El Diablo', this thirst-quencher cocktail certainly won't clear your head, but it may help weaken the malevolent spirit living rent-free in your mind. Handily it's also very easy to make, so if you hear any psychic protests along the lines of 'But I protect you', just grab the crème de cassis, girl, he's lying.

INGREDIENTS

50ml tequila
25ml crème de cassis
25ml lime juice
ginger ale

Glassware: Highball glass

Add the first three ingredients to a highball glass filled with ice. Top with ginger ale and garnish with a lime wedge.

A TOAST
TO
BITTER
RIVALS

SHE'S GOT A CONCEALED WEAPON

THRONE OF GLASS BY SARAH J. MAAS

This high-octane cocktail may appear, at first glance, to be nothing more than a regular girly pink martini, but it's simply playing a part. The concealed weapon here – rather than a career as an assassin carefully hidden from the king's court – is a single shot of absinthe. Underestimate it at your peril.

INGREDIENTS

25ml absinthe
25ml Chambord liqueur
20ml lemon juice
15ml sugar syrup
1 dash Angostura bitters
1 dash Peychaud's bitters
½ egg white

Glassware: Martini glass or Champagne coupe

Add all the ingredients to a cocktail shaker. Shake without ice (dry shake), then add ice and shake again (wet shake). Strain into a chilled glass. Garnish with a twist of lemon zest.

Viscous Little Thing

POWERLESS BY LAUREN ROBERTS

Much like Paedyn Gray and Kai Azer, you'll be
powerless to resist the obvious chemistry between
sharp lime, fiery tequila and the wonderfully smooth,
creamy texture of emulsified egg white in this tequila
sour. A knife to the throat need not be used to gulp
this one down.

INGREDIENTS

50ml tequila
25ml lime juice
20ml sugar syrup
1 egg white

Glassware: Rocks glass

Add all the ingredients to a cocktail shaker. Shake
without ice (dry shake), then add ice and shake again
(wet shake). Strain into a rocks glass over ice.

Once Upon a Bramble Heart

Once Upon a Broken Heart
by Stephanie Garber

This drink is incredibly easy to make, just like the deal Evangeline strikes with the Prince of Hearts to stop her true love marrying another. But unlike cocktails, fairytales aren't so straightforward, especially when a trickster immortal wishes to use you in his dangerous games . . .

Ingredients

60ml gin
30ml lemon juice
15ml sugar syrup
15ml crème de mûre liqueur

Glassware: Rocks glass

Shake the gin, lemon juice and sugar syrup together in a cocktail shaker. Strain into a rocks glass filled with ice. Stir. Add more crushed ice so that the glass is full. Trickle the crème de mûre over the top and garnish with a lemon wedge and a fresh raspberry, to symbolise all of our wounded hearts.

THE BALLAD OF NEGRONI AFTER

THE BALLAD OF NEVER AFTER
BY STEPHANIE GARBER

Having to team up once again with the very person
who stole your chance at happily ever after is a
bitter pill to swallow. Luckily, this is the perfect,
and equally bitter, drink to round off a day of battling
a curse, an untrustworthy partner and your
own desires.

INGREDIENTS

30ml gin
30ml Campari
30ml sweet vermouth

Glassware: Rocks glass

Add all of the ingredients to an ice-filled rocks glass
and stir (one or two large ice cubes are much better
than a load of small ones here). Garnish with an orange
wedge or twist.

GIRL, GODDESS, GIBSON

GIRL, GODDESS, QUEEN BY BEA FITZGERALD

To hell with love and predictably sweet cocktails! If
Persephone can jump head-first into the Underworld
and strong-arm its rude yet frustratingly sexy ruler
Hades, you can enjoy this classic Martini with a
surprisingly tangy twist.

INGREDIENTS

10ml vermouth
60ml gin
Cocktail/silverskin pickled onion

Glassware: Cocktail glass

Fill a mixing glass with ice, add the vermouth and stir to coat the ice. If at this point you want to make a drier Martini, you would strain out some of the vermouth and discard it. Add the gin and stir until chilled and diluted – you want to take some of the 'edge' off the neat gin. Strain into a chilled cocktail glass and defiantly garnish with an onion.

GRUMPY WANTS TEQUILA SUNSHINE

ENCYCLOPAEDIA OF FAERIES
BY HEATHER FAWCETT

This cocktail is as easy to drink as it is easy to make, and while it's not the most sophisticated beverage in the world, it's fun. And sometimes that's exactly what you need. Come on, put away the field journal, suppress the eye roll and observe the charming magic of grenadine and orange juice creating a colour gradient in your glass. We know you want to.

INGREDIENTS

50ml tequila
75ml orange juice
1 bar spoon of grenadine

Glassware: Highball glass

Add the tequila and orange juice to a cocktail shaker. Fill with ice and shake. Strain into a highball glass filled with ice. Pour the grenadine into the top of the glass; it is a dense, sticky syrup and will therefore sink to the bottom, creating the desired sunshine effect.

Brandy Banter

The Song of the Marked
by S. M. Gaither

The Brandy Banter is unique as it is one of very few cocktails where you attend to the elaborate garnish first before the drink itself. So if you're someone who likes their romance precluded by plenty of quick quips and snarky delights, we thoroughly recommend pairing Cas and Elander's adorable dynamic with this sharp sugar-crusted concoction.

Ingredients

50ml Cognac
20ml lemon juice
5ml triple sec
5ml maraschino liqueur
1-2 dashes sugar syrup
2 dashes Boker's Bitters

Glassware: Martini glass or Champagne coupe

Prepare your garnish: find a lemon that fits snugly into the top of the glass you intend to use, and cut a thick wheel around 3cm thick from the middle. Hollow out the middle, removing all of the flesh and the majority of the pith. Place into the glass with around 1cm of peel above the rim (this is why it's important that the lemon peel fits well into the glass). Dip the top of the peel and the glass into some lemon juice, then into sugar to create a sugar rim. If you leave this for a couple of hours, you'll be left with a pretty hard crust of sugar around the rim, which has the advantage of not sweetening your drink too much when you come to drink it; however, it also makes it a little more difficult to clean! Add all the ingredients to a cocktail shaker. Shake hard over ice and double-strain into the prepared glass.

THE GAUNTLET GIMLET

FOURTH WING BY REBECCA YARROS

Officers in the navy adopted the Gimlet as their own
for its vitamin C and ability to be preserved during
long voyages. Similarly, the Gauntlet Gimlet is a
wonderful fortifier for the elite of Navarre's army:
dragon riders. A powerful nip of Dutch courage for
any unlikely squad member, it might just help you
survive the brutal challenges at Basgiath War
College and your fellow murderous cadets.

INGREDIENTS

50ml navy-strength gin
50ml Rose's lime juice cordial

Glassware: Martini glass or Champagne coupe

Add both ingredients to a mixing glass and stir. Strain
into your chilled glass.

THE APEROL SIX

THE ATLAS SIX BY OLIVIE BLAKE

A guaranteed crowd-pleaser, this is a fitting cocktail
to serve your very hot magical secret society. The
below recipe makes a decent-sized glass, but if you
want to make a jug to share with the rest of your
dangerous fellowship, just remember the ratio of
3:2:1 (Prosecco:spirit:soda). So pop the Prosecco
and get pouring – oh dear, are there only five glasses?

INGREDIENTS

75ml Prosecco
50ml Aperol
25ml soda water

Glassware: Any

Add all the ingredients to a glass filled with ice. Stir
and garnish with an orange wedge or slice.

MAGICAL
MANHATTAN

ONE FOR MY ENEMY BY OLIVIE BLAKE

A chance encounter with this cocktail could reignite
a devastating magical conflict the likes of which the
criminal underbelly of Manhattan has never seen
before. Families will be torn apart and sacrifices will
be made. But it will be worth it, because revenge
mixed with this much love has never tasted so sweet.

INGREDIENTS

60ml American whisky: bourbon or rye
20ml sweet vermouth
2-3 dashes bitters

Glassware: Cocktail glass

Fill a mixing glass with ice. Add all of the ingredients and
stir until chilled. Strain into a chilled cocktail glass and
garnish with a maraschino cherry for an extra dash of sweetness and forbidden romance.

FRUITS
OF THE
FAE

BLOODY FAIRY

FAEBOUND BY SAARA EL-ARIFI

An elven warrior may be forgiven for dismissing this classic cocktail as nothing but a strangely savoury relic of the past. Yet the luxurious mouthfeel of tomato juice with the spice of Tabasco and tang of lemon is just perfect for a lazy late brunch or a morning pick-me-up after an exile. The truth is this cocktail has endured for a reason; it's a truly seductive combination of heartening and intoxicating.

INGREDIENTS

50ml vodka

100ml tomato juice

Tabasco sauce (4–10 drops, depending on how hot you want things to get)

Worcestershire sauce (2–5 drops)

A splash of lemon juice

Black pepper (1–2 twists of a pepper grinder)

A pinch of salt (celery salt works well if you have it)

A celery stick (to garnish)

Glassware: Highball glass

Add all the ingredients to a cocktail shaker, but go slowly with the Tabasco and Worcestershire sauces, so you get the spice just how you like it. You might want to play around with the quantity of lemon juice too. Add ice and roll the cocktail shaker, turning it over slowly to allow the ingredients to mix and chill – don't go nuts and shake it as you'll make the drink too watery. Strain into a chilled highball glass, with or without ice. A celery stick is the classic garnish but you can be more inventive and use whatever you have captive in your store cupboard.

ꞋSMASH ME

SHATTER ME BY TAHEREH MAFI

This bourbon cocktail requires a gentle, yet
ultimately lethal touch. Mint and raspberries are
muddled together to form a taste so beautifully
bright and refreshing, even the loneliest of girls
would forget their confines after taking a sip.
Raspberries are preferred but feel free to use any
berry you can (safely) get your hands on.

INGREDIENTS

5–6 berries (raspberries preferred)
6–8 mint leaves
50ml bourbon
25ml lime juice
20ml sugar syrup

Glassware: Highball glass

Gently muddle the raspberries and mint in the bottom
of a cocktail shaker. Be careful not to overly muddle
the mint, as it will bring out bitter flavours from the leaves.
Add the bourbon, lime juice and sugar syrup, along with ice.
Shake and strain into an ice-filled highball glass. Garnish

with a lime wedge or a mint sprig (or both!). If you use a mint sprig, agitate the leaves by slapping the sprig against your hand to release the mint oils and aromas, then place it next to the straw.

THE PRIORY OF THE ORANGE-TINI

THE PRIORY OF THE ORANGE TREE
BY SAMANTHA SHANNON

Whether you're a dragon rider, a secret guard to the Queen or tasked with furthering a thousand-year-old bloodline to protect the realm, this is the ideal cocktail for a woman trying to keep up with life's demands. Marmalade makes this playful martini dangerously drinkable and puts the possibility of love amidst so many spinning plates at an all-time high.

INGREDIENTS

50ml gin
15ml Cointreau
15ml lemon juice
1 bar spoon or teaspoon orange marmalade

Glassware: Martini glass or Champagne coupe

Add all the ingredients to a cocktail shaker. Shake hard over ice and double-strain into a chilled Martini glass or Champagne coupe. Garnish with a strip of zesty orange.

HIGH LADY

A COURT OF MIST AND FURY
BY SARAH J. MAAS

Wedding preparations are well underway and the question of a possible High Lady is on everyone's lips. After all, what would be better to toast to High Fae nuptials with than this classically elegant cocktail?

INGREDIENTS

50ml gin
20ml lemon juice
20ml triple sec
1 egg white (optional)

Glassware: Martini glass or Champagne coupe

Add all the ingredients to a cocktail shaker. Shake without ice (dry shake), then add ice and shake again (wet shake). Strain into a chilled Martini glass or Champagne coupe. Garnish with a strip of lemon peel.

CRESCENT CITY COSMOPOLITAN

HOUSE OF EARTH AND BLOOD
BY SARAH J. MAAS

Do as the Lunathions do and savour every pleasure Crescent City has to offer with this light and cooling Cosmo. Things might get dark, your drink's crimson contents may be spilt (it is the *House of Earth and Blood* after all) but you can always count on a gorgeous fallen angel to help you fight your demons.

INGREDIENTS

30ml vodka
15ml triple sec
15ml lime juice
30ml cranberry juice

Glassware: Martini glass

Put all the ingredients into a cocktail shaker, with some ice. Shake well and strain into a chilled Martini glass. Garnish with a twist of orange zest.

FLAME HOUSE PUNCH

HOUSE OF FLAME AND SHADOW
BY SARAH J. MAAS

If you're ready to really light it up, we highly
recommend the Flame House Punch. This rum-based
cocktail is so strong it might just send you to another
galaxy. If that seems a little unsafe however, follow
Bryce's lead and grip onto the juicy flavour of peach
for some stability.

INGREDIENTS

30ml lemon juice
25ml dark rum
20ml Cognac
10ml peach brandy or crème de pêche
10ml sugar syrup
25ml water

Glassware: Highball glass

Add all the ingredients to a cocktail shaker. Add ice
and shake (be careful to dodge the lightning), then
strain into a highball glass filled with ice.

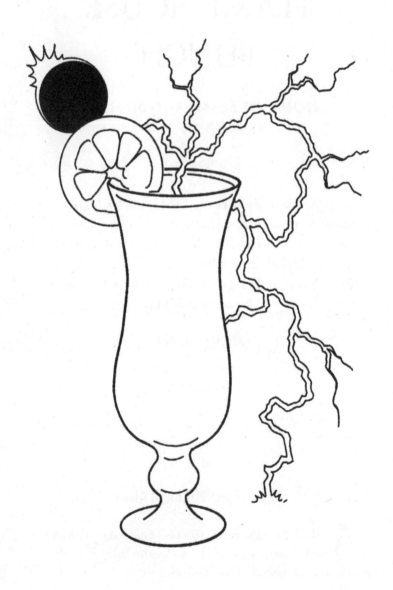

You Hit Me Like a Hurricane

The Hurricane Wars
by Thea Guanzon

In this cocktail, warring forces of light and dark rum combine to create something so intoxicating it may just take down an empire. You may be forgiven for thinking this is just a storm in a tea cup, but trust us, when you first see the magic of dark, sticky grenadine sliding down sunshine yellow fruit juices, the tension will be almost too much to bear. Just ask Talasyn and Alaric.

Ingredients

50ml dark rum
50ml light rum
50ml passion fruit juice
25ml orange juice
12ml fresh lime juice
1 bar spoon grenadine

Glassware: Hurricane or highball glass

Add all the ingredients except for the grenadine to a cocktail shaker. Add ice, shake and strain into a hurricane or highball glass over ice. Pour the grenadine into the top of the glass (it is a dense, sticky syrup and will therefore sink to the bottom with glee). Serve with an orange slice and a maraschino cherry.

PINE AFTER COLADA

THIS WOVEN KINGDOM
BY TAHEREH MAFI

Prince Kamran can't get the beguiling servant girl with the strange eyes out of his head. Who, or what, is she? And what does she have to do with a deadly prophecy that threatens the kingdom? Kamran should know that amidst the infatuation, the burning desire that feels like madness, you've got to have a little light-hearted fun! Luckily, the Pine After Colada provides a wonderfully sweet relief from even the deepest of yearnings.

INGREDIENTS

50ml white rum
50ml coconut cream
150ml pineapple juice

Glassware: Highball or hurricane glass

Add all the ingredients to a cocktail shaker. Add ice and shake well. Strain into a highball or hurricane glass filled with ice. Remember, you've got to have fun with this cocktail, so go wild with garnishes; paper umbrellas, pineapple slices, or perhaps a bejewelled garland of the finest silks might feel more appropriate?

Ninth Cocktail

Ninth House by Leigh Bardugo

This is not the kind of beer cocktail that appears in your average student union bar. Greengages are a type of plum that are sweet and rich; their flavour especially appeals to the kind of privileged palates that might haunt the halls of Yale. The greengage liqueur used in this recipe is made by Bramley & Gage. If you can't get hold of any and wish to survive on campus, then substitute it with a couple of teaspoons of greengage jam – or plum jam if you can bear it.

Ingredients

25ml bourbon
25ml greengage liqueur
15ml lemon juice
10ml agave syrup
50ml ginger ale
lager

Glassware: Highball or half-pint glass

Add the bourbon, greengage liqueur, lemon juice and agave syrup to a cocktail shaker. Add ice and shake well. Strain into a highball or half-pint glass filled with ice. Top with the ginger ale and lager.

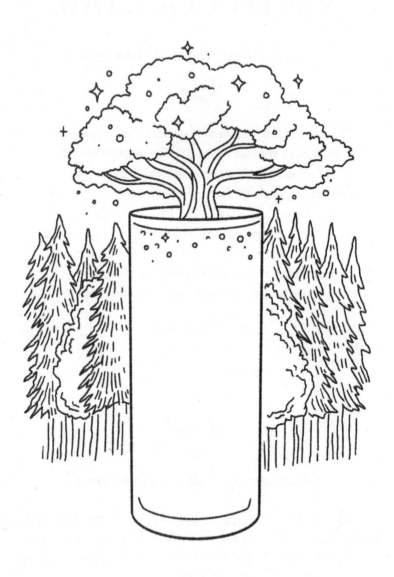

CURSED FOREST MOJITO

WHERE THE DARK STANDS STILL
BY A. B. PORANEK

If you go down to the woods today, you'll find a mojito in disguise. Swapping traditional soda for cherry cola, and the sugar for blackcurrant jam, this sumptuous tipple is so rich in fruity flavour you'll barely notice being whisked away by the demon warden of the wood. But once you're inside his dark crumbling mansion, well, that's another matter.

INGREDIENTS

50ml rum
25ml lemon juice
8 mint leaves
Spoonful of blackcurrant jam
Cherry cola, to top

Glassware: Highball glass

Add the rum, lemon juice, mint leaves and blackcurrant jam to a highball glass. Add crushed ice and churn with a bar spoon. Add cherry cola to top.

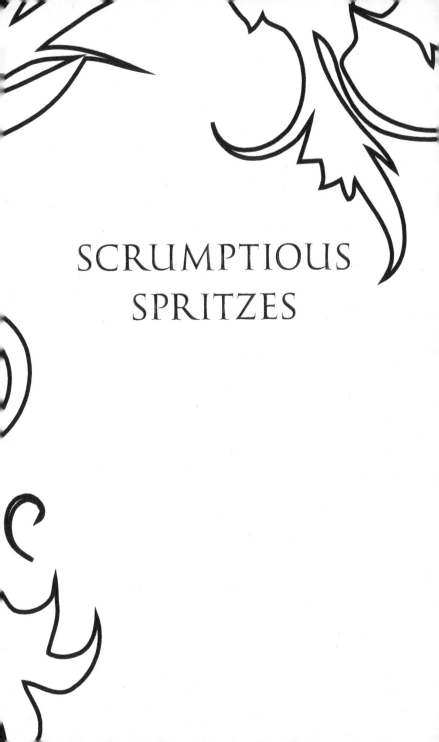

SCRUMPTIOUS
SPRITZES

A COUPE OF THORNS AND ROSÉ

A COURT OF THORNS AND ROSES
BY SARAH J. MAAS

It's the summer solstice party; you're looking
positively fae and its time to let your hair down.
There really is no better beverage for the occasion
than a crisp, sparkling glass of faerie wine. Known
for its euphoric properties, this cocktail will get you
dancing for your High Lord in no time at all.

INGREDIENTS

45ml silver tequila
20ml cranberry juice
15ml lemon juice
10ml sugar syrup
60ml brut rosé sparkling wine, to top

Glassware: Champagne coupe

Add the tequila, cranberry juice, lemon juice and sugar
syrup into a shaker with ice and shake until well-
chilled. Strain into a Champagne coupe. Top with the
sparkling rosé.

MORTAL MULE

CITY OF BONES BY CASSANDRA CLARE

Like *The Mortal Instruments* series, this simple yet
wonderfully layered cocktail has swept the globe.
With a spicy kick from the ginger, a citrus zest from
the lime and a clean booze hit from the vodka, the
Mortal Mule is just as dangerous and irresistible as
the most proficient of demon hunters. A helpful
reminder: if you're making this cocktail in the
hopes of going to bone city and would like that
special someone to rip their clothes off, all you
need to do is ask.

INGREDIENTS

50ml vodka
½ lime, juiced
ginger beer

Glassware: Highball glass or small punch cup

Add the vodka and lime juice to your glass. Fill with
ice and top with ginger beer. You can add Angostura
bitters, if you like an extra herby kick. Add a slice of lime
and a sprig of mint, to garnish.

MOURNING GLORY FIZZ

BELLADONNA BY ADALYN GRACE

Death is inevitable, but as Signa Farrow is here to show us, he's also pretty hot. So instead of moping alone over another guardian's untimely end, why not mix up this cocktail and enjoy a good old-fashioned murder investigation with the gorgeous Grim Reaper himself?

INGREDIENTS

50ml Scotch whisky
25ml lemon/lime juice mix (50:50)
15ml sugar syrup
1 egg white
1–2 dashes absinthe
soda water

Glassware: Highball glass

Add all the ingredients except the soda water to a cocktail shaker. Shake without ice to emulsify the egg white. Add ice and shake again. Strain into a highball glass (no ice), and top up to the top with soda water.

SHAPE-SHIFTER SPRITZ

ZODIAC ACADEMY: THE AWAKENING
BY CAROLINE PECKHAM AND
SUSANNE VALENTI

It can be hard to not break a sweat when an achingly hot dragon shifter has you in his crosshairs. Enter the Shape-shifter Spritz, the only antidote to airs of entitlement, intense gazes and stacked muscles. So let him use you as target practice, this tall drink of elderflower-laced soda water will keep as cool as its cucumber garnish.

INGREDIENTS

35ml Kamm & Sons
15ml elderflower cordial
50ml English sparkling wine
50ml soda water
A wedge of grapefruit

Glassware: Collins glass

Pour all the ingredients over cubed ice in a glass. Stir well. Squeeze a wedge of grapefruit into the cocktail and garnish with a cucumber slice.

THE KIR OF NOTHING

THE QUEEN OF NOTHING BY HOLLY BLACK

Breakups are tough, especially if, like Holly Black's heroine Jude, your wicked faerie king has broken your crown as well as your heart. But even queens of nothing deserve a treat. So stop bingeing reality television, pop the Champagne and pour yourself a drink that's as regal as you are. It's time to grab that bridle and show him who's really in charge.

INGREDIENTS

15ml crème de cassis
Champagne, to top
A fresh raspberry

Glassware: Champagne flute

Pour in the crème de cassis and top with Champagne. Crown with a fresh raspberry.

AMBROSIA

One of the lesser-known classics, the Ambrosia is a glittering Champagne cocktail named after the drink of the gods. According to Greek mythology, any mortal who drank ambrosia became immortal. And after reading what Hades does to Persephone in Katee Robert's red-hot retelling, you'll be on your knees, begging for a sip. We've heard one taste is all you need . . .

INGREDIENTS

25ml Cognac
25ml Calvados
5ml triple sec
5ml lemon juice
Champagne

Glassware: Champagne flute or Champagne coupe

Pour all the ingredients except for the Champagne into a cocktail shaker. Add ice and shake well. Strain into a chilled Champagne flute or Champagne coupe, top up with Champagne and serve immediately.

Scarlet Collins

These Violent Delights
by Chloe Gong

The versatility of a Tom Collins lies in the fact that you can not only mix things up by changing the base spirit (vodka, bourbon, whisky and tequila all work well), but you can also use different sweetening agents. The below version is a fitting tribute to Chloe Gong's Scarlet Gang; it's a cruel crimson beauty that hides the deadly strength of pink gin behind the sweetness of pomegranate and cherry liqueur. We can't think of a more opulent Collins to swear your allegiance to.

Ingredients

50ml pink gin
50ml pomegranate juice
25ml lemon juice
20ml maraschino liqueur
soda water

Glassware: Highball glass

Fill a highball glass with ice. Add the gin, pomegranate juice, lemon juice and maraschino liqueur. Top with soda, add more ice if necessary to fill the glass, and stir to mix. Garnish with a maraschino cherry or, if you've twisted it up using a different liqueur, anything appropriate. Just don't expect your disloyalty to go unpunished.

Hunt Me on Dark and Stormy Waters

Hunt on Dark Waters by Katee Robert

Very difficult to mess up, a Dark and Stormy is the ideal cocktail for anyone who's made one too many mistakes recently, such as stealing from your vampire ex or falling into another realm. It's also a brilliant drink to share with new friends, like the dark band of paladin pirates that have just fished you out of the sea. Make sure to pour an extra-large glass for their telekinetic captain; he looks like he knows his way around a portal.

Ingredients

150ml ginger beer
15ml lime juice
50ml dark rum

Glassware: Highball

Fill a highball glass with ice. Pour in the ginger beer, leaving space for the lime juice and rum. Squeeze in the lime juice then slowly pour over the dark rum to float it on top.

A MARVELLOUS, LIGHT LEMONADE

A MARVELLOUS LIGHT BY FREYA MARSKE

This might not be the most elegant of drinks (those with a more Edwardian sensibility might argue that lemonade is not for grown-ups) and it might seem, well, a bit sour. But, just like Edwin Courcey, it has magical hidden depths. The perfect light and refreshing drink, it deserves to be given a chance.

INGREDIENTS

40ml Jack Daniel's whisky
20ml triple sec
25ml lemon juice
lemonade

Glassware: Highball glass

Add the whisky, triple sec and lemon juice to a cocktail shaker. Add ice and shake well. Strain into a highball glass filled with ice and top with lemonade. Stir gently and garnish with a lemon wheel or wedge.

A TWINKLE OF FROST AND STARLIGHT

A COURT OF FROST AND STARLIGHT
BY SARAH J. MAAS

Just like Sarah J. Maas' refreshing companion tale,
the sweet and sparkling Twinkle is not to be missed.
The incorporation of vodka and Champagne with the
liqueur of snow-white elderflower creates the perfect
cocktail for the Winter Solstice and the opening
of presents (or in Rhysand's case, the undressing
of presents).

INGREDIENTS

25ml vodka
15ml elderflower liqueur or cordial
Champagne (around 75ml)

Glassware: Champagne flute or coupe

Add the vodka and elderflower liqueur to a cocktail shaker. Shake well and double-strain into a chilled Champagne flute or coupe. Top with Champagne. Garnish with a long twist of lemon zest.

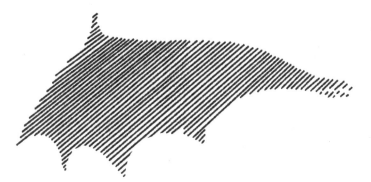

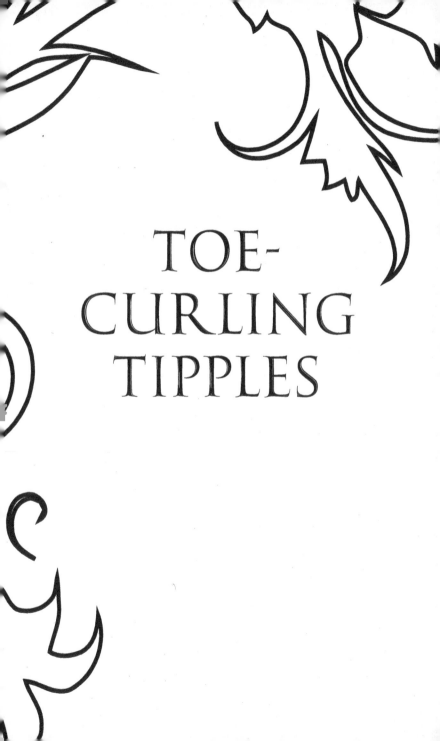

TOE-
CURLING
TIPPLES

HAIR OF THE WOLF

BONDED BY THORNS BY ELIZABETH HELEN

After spending each night as a pack of demonic
wolves, it's really no surprise your four fae princes
are feeling the worse for wear. To break the curse
and get the reverse harem underway (because really,
why should you choose?), prescribe them this spicy
19th-century hangover cure.

INGREDIENTS

15ml Cognac
5ml vinegar (red wine/white wine/cider –
it's up to you)
4–5 dashes Worcestershire sauce
3–5 dashes Tabasco
pinch of salt
pinch of freshly ground black pepper
1 egg yolk

Glassware: Any small glass

Add the Cognac, vinegar, Worcestershire sauce,
Tabasco, salt and pepper to a small glass. Stir to
combine, then crack the egg and separate the yolk before
dropping it into the mixture raw and gobbling down the
whole thing.

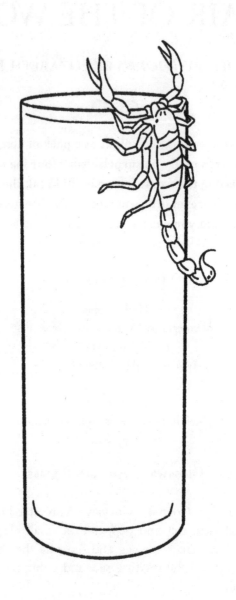

LITTLE SCORPION

THE FAMILIAR BY LEIGH BARDUGO

A cocktail with old-world glamour, the Scorpion was typically served as a punch for several people, garnished with gardenia flowers. The recipe below makes a standalone serving – a Little Scorpion, if you will. But don't worry; it has just as much of a seductive sting, and like Santángel, you won't have the sense to stay away.

INGREDIENTS

50ml white rum
20ml brandy or Cognac
50ml orange juice
30ml lemon juice
20ml orgeat syrup

Glassware: Highball glass

Add all the ingredients to a cocktail shaker. Add ice and shake well before straining into an ice-filled highball glass. Garnish with an edible flower for a touch of romance.

'NOGKILLER

GODKILLER BY HANNAH KANER

Like Kissen, eggnog is a quirky character with history, the cocktail's association with Christmas going all the way back to the 1700s. It's also not the simplest of drinks to get on with, so works better in a group setting as the effort (or angst) per drink is vastly reduced. Perhaps an equally tortured warrior-turned-baker could provide a few mince pies to help this festive love-in along?

INGREDIENTS (SERVES 20)

200g sugar
24 eggs
750ml Cognac
250ml dark rum
1 litre double cream
1 litre full-fat milk

Glassware: Any

Take a large mixing bowl or punchbowl. Whisk the sugar into the eggs and beat in the alcohol. Add the cream and beat again. Add the milk and beat a final time. Ladle into ice-filled glasses. Garnish each glass with freshly grated nutmeg just before serving.

Empyrean Espresso Martini

Iron Flame by Rebecca Yarros

Once in a while there's a cocktail so perfect it's impossible not to imbue it with the unapproachable splendour of heaven itself. No human knows the exact machinations of this fiery meeting of caffeine and vodka, but what we do know is this drink will get you through graduation and possibly a revolution.

INGREDIENTS

50ml vodka
25ml espresso coffee
25ml coffee liqueur
15ml sugar syrup

Glassware: Martini glass

Fill a cocktail shaker with ice. Add all the ingredients and shake until cold. Strain into the prepared Martini glass and add four coffee beans on top.

ALE OF TWIN CITIES

IMMORTAL LONGINGS BY CHLOE GONG

Lime, apple, malted barley, bitters and nettle – they might have competing agendas but when flavours are this jam-packed, you know sparks are going to fly! Trust us, the extra steps are worth it (as they say, San-Er wasn't built in a day). Just think carefully about whose body you're jumping into, or onto afterwards . . .

INGREDIENTS

20ml lime juice
15ml homemade nettle cordial (see below)
75ml cloudy apple juice
15ml malted barley syrup
75ml vodka
25ml Punt e Mes sweet vermouth
2 dashes Angostura bitters

Glassware: Half-pint tankard or glass

Chill a half-pint tankard. Add the lime juice, nettle cordial, apple juice and malted barley syrup to a cocktail shaker or mixing glass. Stir to dissolve the thick malt syrup, then add the alcoholic ingredients, add plenty of ice and shake hard. Strain into the chilled tankard.

FOR THE NETTLE CORDIAL

100g fresh nettle leaves
250g granulated sugar
10g citric acid
200ml water

Wash the nettles, removing any damaged leaves or thick stems, and roughly chop them. Add the sugar, citric acid and water to a saucepan and heat until boiling. Leave to cool to around 70°C. Add the chopped nettles and stir. Once cool, add the mixture to an airtight jar. Leave in a cool, dark place for 1–2 days, agitating or shaking it now and again. Strain through a sieve or piece of muslin if you have it. Add a shot (25ml) or so of vodka to help to preserve the cordial (but only if you're using it for boozy cocktails!) and it will last for 3–4 weeks in the fridge.

Randy
Alexandrian

The Atlas Paradox by Olivie Blake

The Randy Alexandrian is rich and creamy, with
subtle chocolate notes. It's a treat usually best
enjoyed later in the evening, when the hours – or
decades, even – blend together and texts from
exes hold extra potency. But if Olivie Blake's utterly
moreish sequel has taught us anything, it's
that travelling back in time only leads to heartbreak,
so swerve the ex and pour yourself another
drink instead!

Ingredients

45ml brandy
30ml crème de cacao white
30ml double cream

Glassware: Champagne coupe

Fill a cocktail shaker with ice, add all the ingredients and
shake until cold. Strain into a Champagne coupe and
dust with freshly grated nutmeg.

ONE HELL OF A SOUR

HELL BENT BY LEIGH BARDUGO

Sure, it's easy to be cynical. Maybe you want to write off this cocktail as a rich, self-regarding drink that thinks a little too much of itself (why is there egg AND Merlot?!), but once it disappears, you might just find yourself missing what you had. Maybe this devilishly red sour, like Darlington, is well worth going to hell and back for.

INGREDIENTS

60ml whisky, bourbon or rye
25ml lemon juice
20ml sugar syrup
1 egg white
red wine float (fruity reds like Merlot
or Malbec work well)

Glassware: Rocks glass

Add the whisky, lemon juice, sugar syrup and egg white to a cocktail shaker. Shake without ice (dry shake), then add ice and shake again (wet shake). Strain into a rocks glass over ice and gently add the red-wine float.

SAINTS AU CHAMPAGNE

THE CURSE OF SAINTS BY KATE DRAMIS

A slightly naughty and deliciously divine twist on
the Soyer Au Champagne, this is a late-night dessert
cocktail for you to selflessly make your friends,
rivals or love triangle. Blending with the Champagne
aerates the ice cream and makes it so cool and fluffy
it may compel a lover to burn the world down for
you, but alas, that is the curse of saints.

INGREDIENTS (SERVES 4)

240ml cider brandy (Calvados or Cognac will also work)
4 scoops of vanilla ice cream
60ml curaçao (or use triple sec)
60ml sugar syrup
300ml Champagne
Dash of Angostura bitters

Glassware: Champagne coupe

Add all the ingredients aside from the Angostura bitters to a blender and blend on high speed for 10–20 seconds. Pour into Champagne coupes and add a dash of Angostura bitters to each drink.

A VIOLENT END IN THE AFTERNOON

OUR VIOLENT ENDS BY CHLOE GONG

As Juliette and Roma have taught us, there's a fine line between love and hate, between wanting someone dead and wanting to kiss them. Luckily this absinthe-based cocktail really can take the edge off a violent passion, just as the inclusion of citrus handily takes the edge off the absinthe. Just as well when you've got more monsters to battle.

INGREDIENTS

15ml absinthe
20ml lemon juice
10ml sugar syrup
Champagne

Glassware: Champagne flute

Add the absinthe, lemon juice and sugar syrup to a cocktail shaker. Add ice and shake well. Strain into a chilled Champagne flute and top up with Champagne.

WHITE LIES

GODKILLER BY HANNAH KANER

What? you might be thinking. *Coffee, vodka and CREAM?* You hate creamy drinks, always have. But sometimes you just can't predict who or what's going to join your quest. It might be what is essentially a vodka milkshake; it might be an oddly adorable god of white lies. Don't kill either before you give them a chance, and make sure to freshly grate your nutmeg. It makes the cocktail (sorry, Skedi) irresistible.

INGREDIENTS

40ml vodka
20ml coffee liqueur
20ml single or whipping cream

Glassware: Rocks glass

Add the vodka and coffee liqueur to a rocks glass filled with ice. Stir briefly to mix. Slowly pour the cream on top. Garnish with freshly grated nutmeg.

SERIOUS SPICE AND SLOW BURNERS

BLACK VELVET WING

A COURT OF WINGS AND RUIN
BY SARAH J. MAAS

With Champagne shrouded by Guinness, this
cocktail is just as tall, dark and handsome as
everyone's favourite sculpted and tattooed hero,
Rhysand. The heaviness of the stout perfectly
balances out the glittering tartness of the
Champagne. What better way could there
possibly be to seal a death oath with your
bat-winged High Lord?

INGREDIENTS

Champagne
75ml Guinness

Glassware: Champagne flute

Pour the Champagne, then the stout carefully into a
chilled Champagne flute. Stir briefly to mix.

LOVE OR BURNT MARTINI

SERPENT & DOVE BY SHELBY MAHURIN

You're a witch in hiding, he's a huntsman of the Church; the chemistry is just so hot you think you can smell burning. This Love or Burnt Martini is the perfect sensory cocktail for such a union – the navy-strength gin recalls fireworks, and the whisky rinse leaves the lingering sensation of smoke. If you're a fan of big smoky flavours, you won't touch another cocktail again.

INGREDIENTS

5ml (1 teaspoon) smoky scotch whisky
60ml navy-strength gin
15ml dry vermouth

Glassware: Martini glass

Pour the scotch whisky into a Martini glass and swirl it around to rinse the glass before tipping out any excess. Fill a mixing glass with ice and add the gin and vermouth. Stir until chilled, then fine-strain into the prepared Martini glass. For extra spice, you could add the 5ml (1 teaspoon) whisky to the mixing glass with the gin and vermouth, before stirring.

JULEPS ON MINE

A CURSE FOR TRUE LOVE
BY STEPHANIE GARBER

There's nothing more gratifying than a forbidden kiss, but a mint julep might just be the next best thing. It's worth noting that this cocktail is best when you give the mint some time to infuse its tongue-tingling flavour. Waiting may be agony, but you've read two books to get to this point, what's another 10 minutes?

INGREDIENTS

10–12 mint leaves
60ml bourbon
20ml sugar syrup

Glassware: Julep cup or rocks glass

Add all of the ingredients to your chilled julep cup or rocks glass. Stir gently. If possible leave for 10 minutes or so for the mint to infuse. Add crushed ice and churn with a spoon (preferably a bar spoon – the metal disc on one end makes pulling the mint up through the ice super-easy). Top up with more ice and churn again. Finally, cap with ice (in a small mound on top, if you can, for aesthetic reasons), and garnish with a mint sprig or two. You should agitate the mint sprig by slapping it against the back of the hand before placing it into the drink alongside your straws. The key is to make sure every sip is met with a noseful of mint aroma, enhancing the flavour of the cocktail.

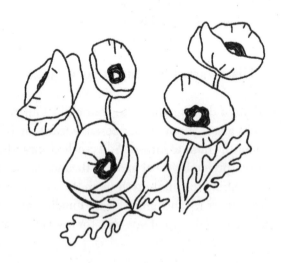

GREEDY G&T

A Court of Silver Flames
by Sarah J. Maas

'Greedy', your mate might murmur, as, like Nesta, you want not one, but two . . . kinds of gin in your G&T. Sloe gin would leave you gasping on its own with tonic so the addition of dry gin lightens this cocktail up to but an iridescent mist. Simple and well balanced, it'll go down extremely easily after a long day of training.

INGREDIENTS

30ml London dry gin
20ml sloe gin
Tonic water, to top

Glassware: Copa de Balon

Fill your glass with ice. Add the dry and sloe gins and top with tonic. Stir, and garnish with a lemon slice and a few juniper berries.

DRAGON'S SCALE ALE

FOURTH WING BY REBECCA YARROS

A blend of gin, lemon juice, ginger syrup and beer, this is a long and refreshing cocktail that pairs perfectly with impenetrable corsets and lightning-hot spice scenes. It's worth taking the time to make your own ginger syrup if you can, as it retains much more of the fiery elements than commercially produced versions. The recipe for the syrup is included below and thankfully doesn't involve any work on the stove, so it'll only be your bedroom at risk of burning down.

INGREDIENTS

40ml gin
50ml lemon juice
50ml ginger syrup (see below)
beer (ale)

Glassware: Pint glass

Add the gin, lemon juice and ginger syrup to a blender with a couple of ice cubes. Blend. Fine-strain the mixture into a chilled pint glass. Top up with beer.

For the ginger syrup

Take 250g peeled and chopped fresh root ginger, 250g caster sugar and 125ml water. Blend together and fine-strain into a bottle to store until needed.

SPICE AND SLOE

THE INADEQUATE HEIR
BY DANIELLE L. JENSEN

For when you're really slammed and just need to get
to the good stuff, does anything scream satisfaction
more than spiced sloe gin spilt into cloudy apple
juice? And like Zarrah and Keris, if one drink isn't
enough for you, feel free to go again with the
warm version. It's guaranteed to heat up even the
coldest of hearts.

INGREDIENTS

Cloudy apple juice
60ml spiced sloe gin

Glassware: Old-Fashioned glass

Fill your glass with ice. Add cloudy apple juice, leaving
just enough room at the top for the gin. Use a spoon to
float the gin on top.

You could also drink this as a warm cocktail – add the
cloudy apple juice to a saucepan and put over a medium heat.
Heat until the juice is warm (but not boiling) and take off the
heat. Pour the juice into a mug and add the gin.

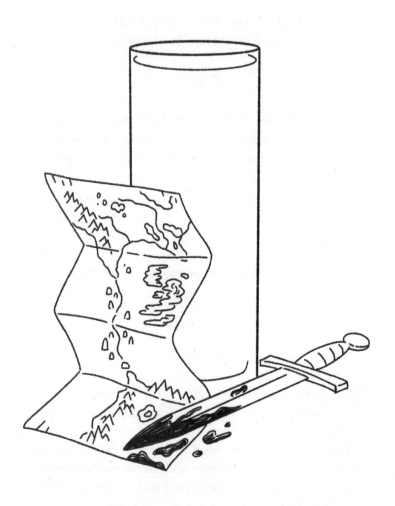

SLOE BURN

THE BRIDGE KINGDOM
BY DANIELLE L. JENSEN

The catch with this drink is that it requires a very long shake, but you'll be rewarded with a delicious, soufflé-like texture. We know what you're thinking, what's the point of keeping things light and fluffy? But to truly appreciate that first sip, you've got to build the tension of the foam; will it come to a head above the glass, will it simply overflow? Not everything will be on your terms, but that's what makes it truly delicious.

INGREDIENTS

60ml sloe gin
20ml whole milk (or use any milk substitute)
15ml lemon juice
10ml lime juice
10ml sugar syrup
1 egg white
30ml soda water

Glassware: Highball glass (a straight-sided highball glass will work best)

Fill a cocktail shaker with ice. Add all the ingredients, except for the soda water, and shake for 7 minutes (wrap a tea towel around the shaker to stop it getting too cold to hold). It's not necessary to shake non-stop for 7 minutes, just for 7 minutes total. Try and team up with another person, if possible, for the long shake, to lighten the load. Once shaken, leave the shaker to rest for around 2 minutes.

Strain the cocktail into the highball glass at the same time as pouring the soda; this will create a fizzy and foamy effect. Make sure you open the shaker first over the sink so the cocktail doesn't pour out everywhere. Fill the glass until about three-quarters full. Put the glass in the fridge for 1 minute, letting the foam settle and get cold. Remove the glass and make a hole in the middle of the foam with a straw. Pour the remaining cocktail into the hole so that the foam rises up the glass. You are aiming to get a couple of centimetres of foam head above the glass.

BLOOD AND SMUT

FROM *BLOOD AND ASH* BY
JENNIFER L. ARMENTROUT

It's no shock that the combination of poppy-red cherry brandy and golden orange juice creates a cocktail guaranteed to make your first night, or perhaps any night, special. Take the following as a warning . . .or a promise; like all the most alluring drinks, it's strictly not for maidens.

INGREDIENTS

25ml Scotch whisky
25ml sweet vermouth
25ml cherry brandy
25ml orange juice

Glassware: Martini glass or Champagne coupe

Add all the ingredients to a cocktail shaker. Shake over ice and strain into a chilled Martini glass or Champagne coupe.

Garnish with a maraschino cherry or, if you're really fired up, a flambéed piece of orange zest. To flambé the orange zest, first cut a large(ish) disc of zest from an orange. Make sure there isn't too much pith on the underside of the zest. Hold it between your fingers, peel-side facing the glass. Take a lighter and hold it between the zest and the drink. In one movement, squeeze the zest to release the oils, which will sparkle in the lighter's flame. Discard the zest and your duties.

HOUSE OF HANKY PANKY

HOUSE OF SKY AND BREATH
BY SARAH J. MAAS

A sweeter, lighter version of a martini, the House of
Hanky Panky is served straight up, which makes it
the perfect accompaniment for Maas' breathtaking,
straight-to-the-smut sequel. Take a sip and
gallop like a gorgeous long-legged faun towards
the scene with Ruhn's lip ring; it's less than
100 pages, thank Gods.

INGREDIENTS

30ml sweet vermouth
30ml gin
2 dashes Fernet-Branca

Glassware: Martini glass or Champagne coupe

Put all the ingredients into a mixing glass with ice.
Stir. Strain into a chilled glass and garnish with a
strip of orange zest.

DRAGON MARGARIDER

IRON FLAME BY REBECCA YARROS

This a cocktail you fight for, that you fly eight hours straight for without even stopping to get your leathers. The key to making it great is using fresh lime juice, squeezed by hand just before it's needed. To get the most out of the fruit, roll it repeatedly against the stone bench of a steamy bathing chamber, or any flat surface you have to hand, before squeezing. Forget dragons, this will be the ride of your life.

INGREDIENTS

50ml tequila
30ml lime juice
25ml triple sec or curaçao

Glassware: Martini glass

Shake all the ingredients with ice and double-strain into a Martini glass with a salted rim. Garnish with a lime wheel or wedge on the side of the glass.

Romantasy Checklist

Consider yourself a romantasy connoisseur? Use this list of the most heart-hammering novels to keep track of how many you've read, and how many cocktails you've drunk.

Book	Cocktail
○ *From Blood and Ash* by Jennifer L. Armentrout	○ Blood and Smut (p. 139)
○ *Shadow and Bone* by Leigh Bardugo	○ Fine, Make Me Your Vesper (p. 23)
○ *Ninth House* by Leigh Bardugo	○ Ninth Cocktail (p. 71)
○ *Hell Bent* by Leigh Bardugo	○ One Hell of a Sour (p. 113)

◑ *The Familiar* by Leigh Bardugo	◑ Little Scorpion (p.103)
◑ *The Cruel Prince* by Holly Black	◑ The Cruel Quince Daiquiri (p. 13)
◑ *The Wicked King* by Holly Black	◑ The Wicked Sling (p. 15)
◑ *The Queen of Nothing* by Holly Black	◑ The Kir of Nothing (p. 83)
◑ *One For My Enemy* by Olivie Blake	◑ Magical Manhattan (p. 49)
◑ *The Atlas Six* by Olivie Blake	◑ The Aperol Six (p. 47)
◑ *The Atlas Paradox* by Olivie Blake	◑ Randy Alexandrian (p. 111)
◑ *The Serpent and The Wings of Night* by Carissa Broadbent	◑ Vampiro (p.17)
◑ *City of Bones* by Cassandra Clare	◑ Mortal Mule (p. 79)
◑ *The Curse of Saints* by Kate Dramis	◑ Saints Au Champagne (p. 115)
◑ *Faebound* by Saara El-Arifi	◑ Bloody Fairy (p. 53)
◑ *Emily Wilde's Encyclopaedia of Fairies* by Heather Fawcett	◑ Grumpy Wants Tequila Sunshine (p. 41)
◑ *Girl, Goddess, Queen* by Bea Fitzgerald	◑ Girl, Goddess, Gibson (p. 39)

- *The Song of the Marked* by S. M. Gaither
- *Once Upon a Broken Heart* by Stephanie Garber
- *The Ballad of Never After* by Stephanie Garber
- *A Curse for True Love* by Stephanie Garber
- *One Dark Window* by Rachel Gillig
- *These Violent Delights* by Chloe Gong
- *Our Violent Ends* by Chloe Gong
- *Immortal Longings* by Chloe Gong
- *Belladonna* by Adalyn Grace
- *The Hurricane Wars* by Thea Guanzon
- *Bride* by Ali Hazelwood
- *Bonded by Thorns* by Elizabeth Helen

- Brandy Banter (p. 42)
- Once Upon a Bramble Heart (p. 35)
- The Ballad of Negroni After (p. 37)
- Juleps on Mine (p. 127)
- The Devil Within Me (p. 27)
- Scarlet Collins (p. 87)
- A Violent End in the Afternoon (p. 117)
- Ale of Twin Cities (p. 108)
- Mourning Glory Fizz (p. 80)
- You Hit Me Like a Hurricane (p. 67)
- Old-Fashioned Alpha Male (p. 9)
- Hair of the Wolf (p. 101)

- *The Bridge Kingdom* by Danielle L. Jensen
- A Sloe Burn (p. 137)

- *The Inadequate Heir* by Danielle L. Jensen
- Spice and Sloe (p. 135)

- *Godkiller* by Hannah Kaner
- 'Nogkiller (p. 105)

- White Lies (p. 118)

- *Gild* by Raven Kennedy
- Mai Tai-rant (p. 21)

- *Throne of Glass* by Sarah J. Maas
- She's Got a Concealed Weapon (p. 31)

- *A Court of Thorns and Roses* by Sarah J. Maas
- A Coupe of Thorns and Rose (p. 77)

- Green-eyed Fairy (p. 25)

- *A Court of Mist and Fury* by Sarah J. Maas
- High Lady (p. 61)

- *A Court of Wings and Ruin* by Sarah J. Maas
- Black Velvet Wing (p. 123)

- *A Court of Frost and Starlight* by Sarah J. Maas
- A Twinkle of Frost and Starlight (p. 95)

- *A Court of Silver Flames* by Sarah J. Maas
- Greedy G&T (p. 131)
- *House of Earth and Blood* by Sarah J. Maas
- Crescent City Cosmopolitan (p. 63)
- *House of Sky and Breath* by Sarah J. Maas
- House of Hanky Panky (p. 143)
- *House of Flame and Shadow* by Sarah J. Maas
- Flame House Punch (p. 65)
- *Shatter Me* by Tahereh Mafi
- Smash Me (p. 55)
- *This Woven Kingdom* by Tahereh Mafi
- Pine After Colada (p. 69)
- *Serpent & Dove* by Shelby Mahurin
- Love or Burnt Martini (p. 125)
- *A Marvellous Light* by Freya Marske
- A Marvellous, Light Lemonade (p. 93)
- *Ledge* by Stacey McEwan
- Beast Between The Sheets (p. 19)
- *Zodiac Academy: The Awakening* by Caroline Peckham and Susanne Valenti
- Shape-shifter Spritz (p. 81)
- *Where the Dark Stands Still* by A. B. Poranek
- Cursed Forest Mojito (p. 73)

- *Neon Gods* by Katee Robert
- Ambrosia (p. 85)
- *Hunt on Dark Waters* by Katee Robert
- Hunt Me on Dark and Stormy Waters (p. 89)
- *Powerless* by Lauren Roberts
- Viscous Little Thing (p. 33)
- *The Priory of The Orange Tree* by Samantha Shannon
- The Priory of the Orange-tini (p. 59)
- *A Court this Cruel and Lovely* by Stacia Stark
- Morally Greyhound (p. 11)
- *Fourth Wing* by Rebecca Yarros
- The Gauntlet Gimlet (p. 45)
- Dragon's Scale Ale (p. 133)
- *Iron Flame* by Rebecca Yarros
- Empyrean Espresso Martini (p. 107)
- Dragon Margarider (p. 144)

Credits

WHAT TO SERVE YOUR SHADOW KING

Bride by Ali Hazelwood, Little, Brown Book Group, 2024

A Court this Cruel and Lovely by Stacia Stark, Bingeable Books LLC, 2023

The Cruel Prince by Holly Black, Hot Key Books, 2018

The Wicked King by Holly Black, Hot Key Books 2019

The Serpent and the Wings of Night by Carissa Broadbent, Tor Publishing Group, 2023

Ledge by Stacey McEwan, Angry Robot Books, 2022

Gild by Raven Kennedy, Penguin Books, 2020

Shadow and Bone by Leigh Bardugo, Indigo, 2012

A Court of Thorns and Roses by Sarah J. Maas, Bloomsbury, 2015

One Dark Window by Rachel Gillig, Bloomsbury, 2022

A TOAST TO BITTER RIVALS

Throne of Glass by Sarah J. Maas, Bloomsbury, 2012

Powerless by Lauren Roberts, Simon & Schuster, 2023

Once Upon a Broken Heart by Stephanie Garber, Hodder & Stoughton, 2021

The Ballad of Never After by Stephanie Garber, Hodder & Stoughton, 2022

Girl, Goddess, Queen by Bea Fitzgerald, Penguin Books, 2023

Emily Wilde's Encyclopaedia of Fairies by Heather Fawcett, Little, Brown Book Group, 2023

The Song of the Marked by S. M. Gaither, Yellow Door Publishing INC, 2020

Fourth Wing by Rebecca Yarros, Little, Brown Group, 2023

The Atlas Six by Olivie Blake, Tor Publishing Group, 2022

One For My Enemy by Olivie Blake, Tor Publishing Group, 2023

FRUITS OF THE FAE

Faebound by Saara El-Arifi, HarperCollins Publishers, 2024

Shatter Me by Tahereh Mafi, Electric Monkey, 2018

The Priory of The Orange Tree by Samantha Shannon, Bloomsbury, 2019

A Court of Mist and Fury by Sarah J. Maas, Bloomsbury, 2016

House of Earth and Blood by Sarah J. Maas, Bloomsbury, 2020

House of Flame and Shadow by Sarah J. Maas, Bloomsbury, 2024

The Hurricane Wars by Thea Guanzon, HarperCollins Publishers, 2023

This Woven Kingdom by Tahereh Mafi, HarperCollins Publishers, 2022

Ninth House by Leigh Bardugo, Gollancz, 2019

Where the Dark Stands Still by A. B. Poranek, Penguin Books, 2024

SCRUMPTIOUS SPRITZES

A Court of Thorns and Roses by Sarah J. Maas, Bloomsbury, 2015

City of Bones by Cassandra Clare, Walker Books, 2007

Belladonna by Adalyn Grace, Hodder & Stoughton, 2022

Zodiac Academy: The Awakening by Caroline Peckham and Susanne Valenti, self-published, 2019

The Queen of Nothing by Holly Black, Hot Key Books 2019

Neon Gods by Katee Robert, SourceBooks, 2021

These Violent Delights by Chloe Gong, Hodder & Stoughton, 2020

Hunt on Dark Waters by Katee Robert, Del Rey, 2023

A Marvellous Light by Freya Marske, Tor Publishing Group, 2021

A Court of Frost and Starlight by Sarah J. Maas, Bloomsbury, 2018

TOE-CURLING TIPPLES

Bonded by Thorns by Elizabeth Helen, Luna Fox Press, 2023

The Familiar by Leigh Bardugo, Penguin Books, 2024

Godkiller by Hannah Kaner, HarperCollins Publishers, 2023

Iron Flame by Rebecca Yarros, Little, Brown Group, 2023

Immortal Longings by Chloe Gong, Hodder & Stoughton, 2023

The Atlas Paradox by Olivie Blake, Tor Publishing Group, 2022

Hell Bent by Leigh Bardugo, Gollancz, 2023

The Curse of Saints by Kate Dramis, Michael Joseph, 2023

Our Violent Ends by Chloe Gong, Hodder & Stoughton, 2020

SERIOUS SPICE AND SLOW BURNERS

A Court of Wings and Ruin by Sarah J. Maas, Bloomsbury, 2017

Serpent & Dove by Shelby Mahurin, HarperCollins Publishers, 2019

A Curse for True Love by Stephanie Garber, Hodder & Stoughton, 2023

A Court of Silver Flames by Sarah J. Maas, Bloomsbury, 2021

Fourth Wing by Rebecca Yarros, Little, Brown Group, 2023

The Inadequate Heir by Danielle L. Jensen, Penguin Books, 2022

The Bridge Kingdom by Danielle L. Jensen, Penguin Books, 2022

From Blood and Ash by Jennifer L. Armentrout, Blue Box Press, 2020

House of Sky and Breath by Sarah J. Maas, Bloomsbury, 2022

Iron Flame by Rebecca Yarros, Little, Brown Group, 2023

This or That

What are your Romantasy preferences? Answer these alone or share it with your book club (perhaps with a delicious drink in hand) to find out . . .

This	That
◑ *Fated Mates*	◑ Enemies to Lovers
◑ *Forbidden Love*	◑ Cross-species
◑ *Love Triangles*	◑ Secret Identity
◑ *Grumpy*	◑ Sunshine
◑ *True Love's Kiss*	◑ Reluctant Companions

- ◐ Alpha Male
- ◐ Girl Boss
- ◐ Forced Proximity
- ◐ Resurrection
- ◐ Shadow King
- ◐ Crusader
- ◐ Found Family
- ◐ Transformation

Reading Journal

U se these pages to make notes on your favourite
novels. How many can you race through this
year?

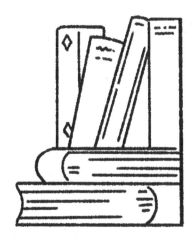

TITLE:

AUTHOR:

OVERALL RATING:

SPICE LEVEL:

FAVOURITE CHARACTER:

FAVOURITE CHAPTER:

FAVOURITE QUOTE:

PLOT SUMMARY:

TITLE:

AUTHOR:

OVERALL RATING:

SPICE LEVEL:

FAVOURITE CHARACTER:

FAVOURITE CHAPTER:

FAVOURITE QUOTE:

PLOT SUMMARY:

TITLE:

AUTHOR:

OVERALL RATING:

SPICE LEVEL:

FAVOURITE CHARACTER:

FAVOURITE CHAPTER:

FAVOURITE QUOTE:

PLOT SUMMARY:

TITLE:

AUTHOR:

OVERALL RATING:

SPICE LEVEL:

FAVOURITE CHARACTER:

FAVOURITE CHAPTER:

FAVOURITE QUOTE:

PLOT SUMMARY:

TITLE:

AUTHOR:

OVERALL RATING:

SPICE LEVEL:

FAVOURITE CHARACTER:

FAVOURITE CHAPTER:

FAVOURITE QUOTE:

PLOT SUMMARY:

TITLE:

AUTHOR:

OVERALL RATING:

SPICE LEVEL:

FAVOURITE CHARACTER:

FAVOURITE CHAPTER:

FAVOURITE QUOTE:

PLOT SUMMARY:

Pop Press is an imprint of Ebury Publishing
20 Vauxhall Bridge Road
London SW1V 2SA

Pop Press is part of the Penguin Random House group of companies
whose addresses can be found at global.penguinrandomhouse.com

First published by Pop Press in 2024

www.penguin.co.uk

A CIP catalogue record for this book is available from the British Library

ISBN 9781529945065

Writer: Alice Johnstone
Illustrator: Ollie Mann

Typeset in 12/18pt Horley Old Style MT Pro by
Jouve (UK), Milton Keynes
Printed and bound in Great Britain by Clays Ltd, Elcograf S.p.A.

The authorised representative in the EEA is Penguin Random House
Ireland, Morrison Chambers, 32 Nassau Street, Dublin D02 YH68